OCS Study MMS 2006-003

Development of Airborne Remote Sensing Methods for Surveys of Pacific Walrus

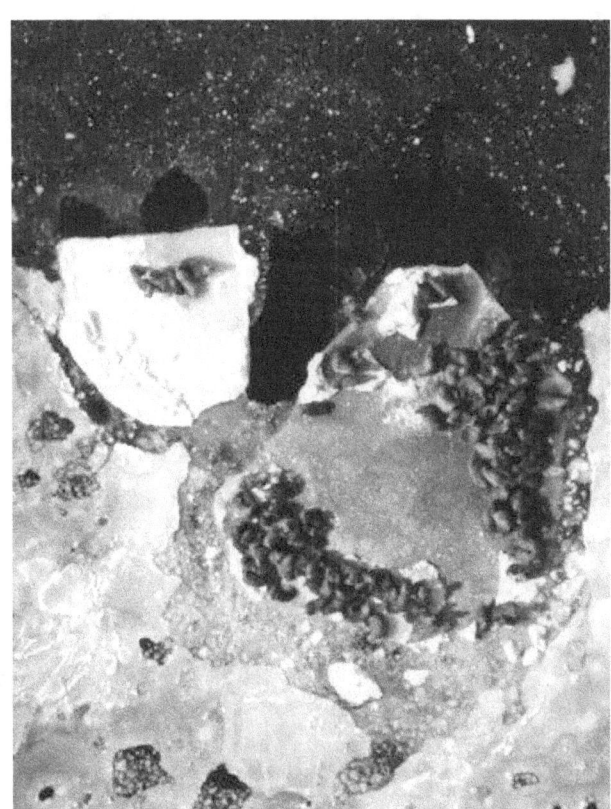 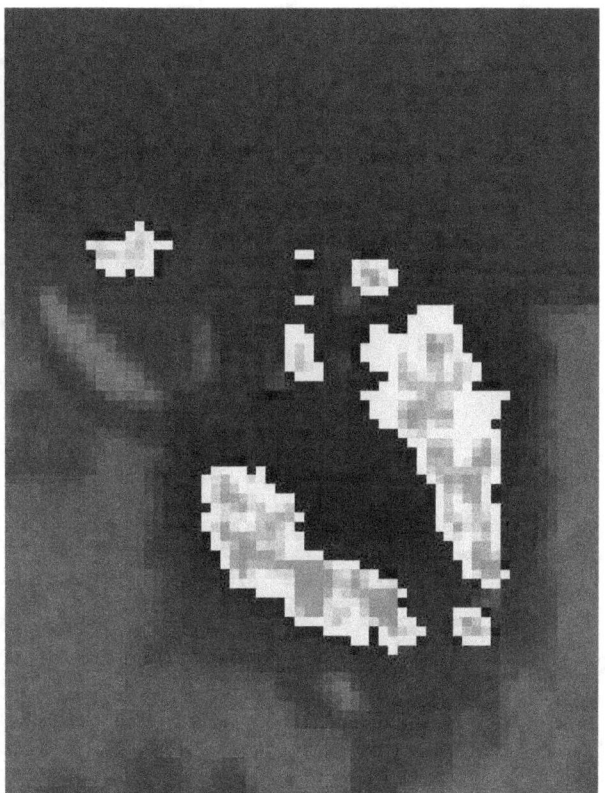

Prepared for:

U.S. Department of the Interior
Minerals Management Service
Alaska Outer Continental Shelf Region

OCS Study MMS 2006-003

Final Report:

Development of Airborne Remote Sensing Methods for Surveys of Pacific Walruses

by:

Douglas M. Burn[1], Mark S. Udevitz[2], Marc A. Webber[3] and Joel L. Garlich-Miller[1]

[1]U.S. Fish and Wildlife Service, Marine Mammals Management,
1011 East Tudor Road, Anchorage, AK 99503

[2]U.S. Geological Survey, Alaska Science Center,
1011 East Tudor Road, Anchorage, AK 99503

[3]U.S. Fish and Wildlife Service, Muscatatuck National Wildlife Refuge,
12589 E. U.S. Highway 50, Seymour, IN 47274

This study was funded in part by the U.S. Department of the Interior, Minerals Management Service (MMS), Alaska Outer Continental Shelf Region, Anchorage, Alaska, through Intra-agency Agreement No. 0103RU72398, with the U.S. Fish and Wildlife Service, as part of the MMS Alaska Environmental Studies Program.

December 2006

Table of Contents

List of Tables iii

List of Figures iii

Abstract iv

Introduction 1

    Methods 2

        Study area and survey dates 2

        Remote sensing systems 3

        Survey aircraft 4

        Flight crew 5

        Flight operations 6

        Analytical methods 6

Results...
.... 10

Discussion 14

Discussion 14

Acknowledgments 16

Study Products 16

Literature Cited 18

Appendix 1. Scanner specifications 20

Appendix 2. Total walrus heat measured for each walrus hotspot recorded 22

List of Tables

Table 1. Survey blocks and transects flown...12

Table 2. Total walrus heat measured for each walrus hotspot recorded with corresponding
walrus counts from digital aerial photography..13

Table 3. Abundance estimates for survey blocks..13

List of Figures

Figure 1. Study area for field data collection of AMS thermal imagery and digital aerial
photography indicating survey blocks, midlines of strip transects flown and the
location of detected walrus groups..3

Figure 2. Aero Commander 690B turbine engine aircraft. 4

Figure 3. Survey flight crew. Pictured left to right are: William Baker (scanner operator),
Douglas Burn (walrus observer and flight coordinator), Marc Webber (walrus observer
and camera operator), and Ralph Aiken (pilot)...5

Figure 4. Diagram of survey aircraft indicating the location of flight crew and the configuration
of the remote sensing systems...5

Figure 5. Example of frequency histogram of AMS thermal imagery showing temperature
threshold between the background environment and walruses that occurs at -2.81°C.
Pixels to the right of the threshold value have some portion of their area covered by
walruses. The major peaks of the histogram correspond to environmental features such
as thick, snow-covered ice, and bare ice of varying thickness..7

Figure 6. Poisson regression of walrus counts as a function of total heat index for AMS thermal
imagery at 4 m spatial resolution. See text for model details. 11

Abstract

In April 2003, we conducted an operational test of an airborne multispectral scanner (AMS) over pack ice in the Bering Sea to evaluate the potential of this system as a survey tool for Pacific walruses. We scanned a total of 28,875 km^2 of sea ice habitat at a spatial resolution of 4 m and collected high resolution photographs from a subset of the thermally detected walrus groups. We found a significant positive relationship between walrus group size and the amount of heat measured by the AMS and used this relationship to estimate total walrus numbers in the survey area. The number of walruses hauled out onto sea ice in our study area was estimated at 4,785 animals with a 95% confidence interval of 2,499–7,111. We believe that the AMS system as configured for this study would be a highly effective tool for surveying large areas of sea ice habitat for walrus groups. With a 6 km swath width, it should be possible to sample more 10,000 km^2 in an 8-hr flight. Although walrus groups > 4 animals were easily detected and enumerated in the 4 m thermal data, the system was unable to detect individual walruses or seals (*Phoca spp.* and *Erignathus barbatus*). We found that most (94.6%) of the walruses photographed in our survey area occurred in groups > 6 animals, therefore we expect the magnitude of any bias due to undetected groups of hauled out animals would be relatively small.

Introduction

The last population survey of Pacific walrus (*Odobenus rosmarus divergens*) was conducted jointly by the United States and the Soviet Union in 1990 (Gilbert *et al.* 1992) and after nearly 15 years, the current population size is unknown. The technique used at that time, a visual aerial survey, is now considered to be inadequate for measuring population size with sufficient precision to monitor trend (Hills and Gilbert 1994, Gilbert 1999). Drawbacks to a visual aerial survey include: a narrow survey swath width, observer bias and fatigue, the lack of a permanent data record, and safety concerns associated with low-level flight in remote areas. Of these, narrow survey swath width is considered to have the greatest impact on the precision of the resulting population estimate due to the large geographic area that must be surveyed in a short time period (Estes and Gilbert 1978, Gilbert 1999). At an international workshop of walrus biologists held by the United States Fish and Wildlife Service (USFWS) and the United States Geological Survey (USGS), the consensus opinion was that remote sensing techniques capable of collecting data over large areas should be investigated and developed as an alternative to visual surveys (Garlich-Miller and Jay 2000).

The history of aerial surveys of Pacific walrus has been reviewed by Hills and Gilbert (1994), Gilbert (1999), and Udevitz *et al.* (2001). In the fall season when most of the previous surveys were conducted, the walrus population is segregated, with some animals associated with the ice edge in the Chukchi Sea, while others make use of terrestrial haulouts along the coast of Bristol Bay, Alaska in the United States, and the Chukotka and Kamchatka peninsulas in Russia. Fewer surveys have been conducted in the winter and early spring, when the entire walrus population occurs almost exclusively on the pack ice of the Bering Sea with concentrations in the Gulf of Anadyr, south-west of St. Lawrence Island, and south of Nunivak Island (Fay 1982).

At any time of year, some or all of the walrus population is associated with sea ice, where animals haul out of the water and rest in large aggregations on ice floes (Fay 1982). Within minutes of leaving the water, their skin temperature becomes noticeably warmer than the background environment (Ray and Fay 1968), which provides excellent thermal contrast. In the mid-1970s, Wartzok and Ray (1980) experimented with a variety of aerial photography and remote sensing techniques, including thermal imagery, to detect marine mammals in the Bering Sea. While their results were promising, the development of a survey method using thermal imagery was not feasible due to limitations of existing technology. Over a decade later, Barber *et al.* (1991) used a forward-looking infrared system (FLIR) to demonstrate that groups of Atlantic walrus (*Odobenus rosmarus rosmarus*) can be detected by their signatures in the 8-12μm thermal infrared (IR) band. In addition to FLIR systems, there are other types of thermal imagery systems available for survey applications. In contrast to the video image of FLIR systems, across-track thermal scanners are capable of producing a continuous vertical photo-like digital image in the thermal IR band.

In April 2002, we tested an Airborne Multispectral Scanner (AMS) to determine if this technology could be used to detect walrus groups on sea ice and estimate the number of walrus present in each group (Burn *et al.* 2006). We collected thermal imagery of 37 walrus groups in the Bering Sea at spatial resolutions ranging from 1-4 m, and high resolution digital photographs of the same walrus groups. We found that walrus were considerably warmer than the background environment of ice, snow, and seawater and easily detected in the thermal imagery. We also found a significant linear relation between walrus group size and the amount of heat measured by the thermal sensor at all 4 spatial resolutions tested. We hypothesized that the relationship between group size and thermal signature could be used in a double-sampling framework to estimate total walrus numbers in an area, by conducting a thermal survey of an area and obtaining photographs from a sub sample of the thermally detected groups.

Based upon the successful test of the AMS system in 2002, we proposed conducting a pilot survey for Pacific walrus in the spring of 2003 in the Bering Sea pack ice near St Lawrence Island. The study area was selected because major aggregations of walruses typically occur during spring in association with polynyas that form around the Island (Fay 1982). The objectives of our study were to:

1. Conduct a full operational test of the AMS system to evaluate the potential of this system as a survey tool for Pacific walruses distributed over a wide geographic area.
2. Evaluate the effectiveness of the AMS system as a survey tool for other marine mammal and bird species.

Methods

Study area and survey dates

Our study area consisted of the Bering Sea pack ice near St. Lawrence Island, Alaska (Figure 1). The area is characterized by a re-occurring Polynya and known to support large concentrations of Pacific walruses during the late winter-early spring breeding season (Fay 1982). Our logistical base for the study was Nome, Alaska. We were based in Nome from March 30 through April 15, 2003, and were able to fly surveys on clear weather days from April 5-10, 2003.

The study area was partitioned into seven survey bocks (Figure 1) and each survey block was partitioned into strip transects with midlines spaced 6 km apart. The spacing of transects allowed total coverage of the survey block without overlap. We use the terms "transect" and "strip transect" interchangeably - the survey aircraft flew along the midlines of selected strip transects. Block size was designed with the goal of sampling 30% of each block, and was influenced by the operational range of the aircraft and the distance of the survey block from Nome. Transects were oriented north-south and surveyed from west to east so that survey effort could be finished as close to Nome as possible.

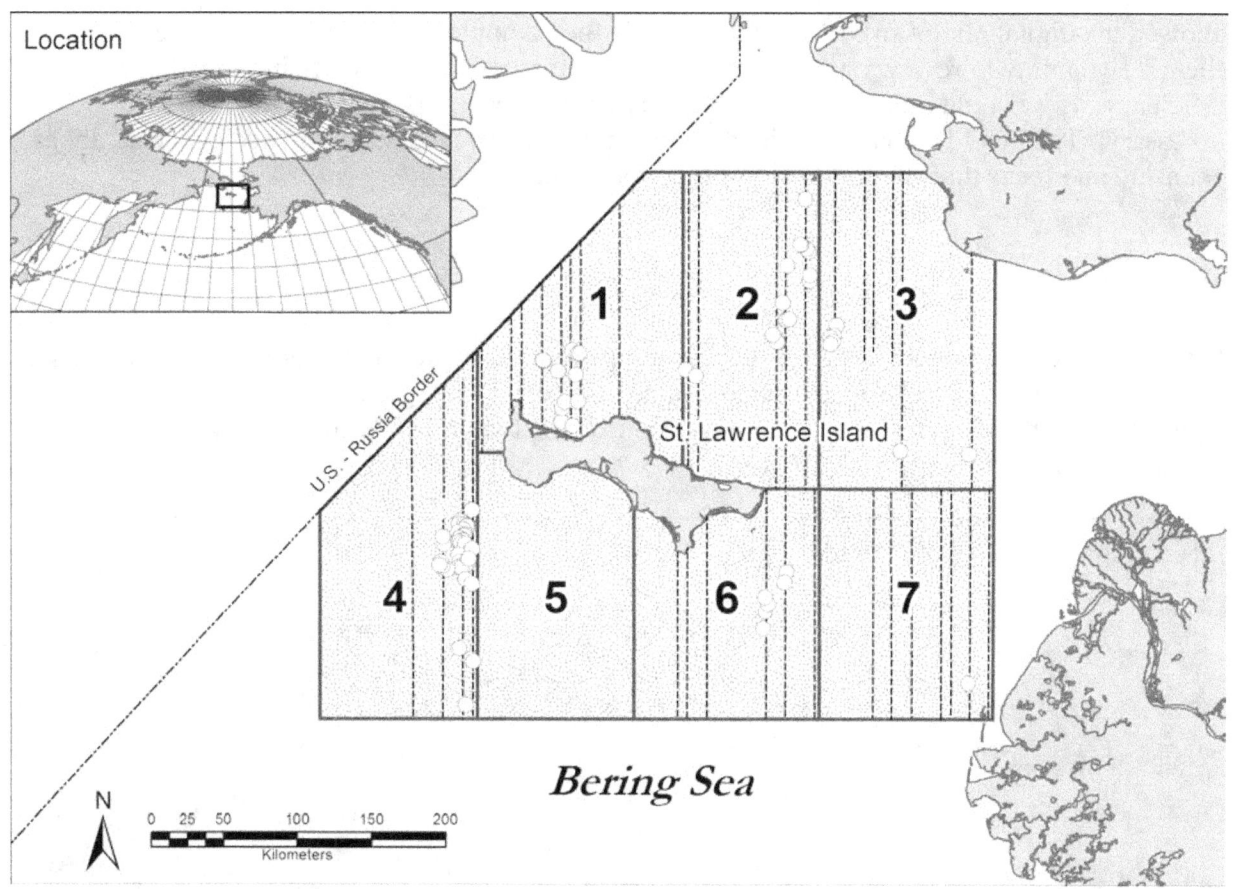

Figure 1. Study area for field data collection of AMS thermal imagery and digital aerial photography indicating survey blocks, midlines of strip transects flown and the location of detected walrus groups.

Remote sensing systems

We used a Daedelus Airborne Multispectral Scanner (AMS), built by SenSyTech Inc. (now Argon ST) of Ann Arbor, Michigan (Appendix 1). The system has a 1.25 milliradian instantaneous field of view (IFOV) and collects imagery across a sensor array 1,440 pixels wide. When the data are corrected for tangential distortion, the resulting image is 1,493 pixels wide. We recorded 6 unique spectral channels of information, with at least one channel in the thermal infrared (8.5-12.5µm) range. Each channel was recorded with 12-bit radiometric resolution (able to discriminate 2^{12}, i.e. 4,096 different temperature levels). Similar to most passive remote sensing systems, the AMS was unable see through clouds and fog, and could only be operated in clear weather conditions.

We used a Nikon D1X camera to collect high-resolution digital photographs of walrus groups. This 5.47 megapixel camera produced images with dimensions of 3,008 x 1,960 pixels. The camera was connected to a notebook computer equipped with Nikon Capture software via an IEEE 1394 (firewire) port. The use of the notebook computer and camera control software allowed the digital photos to be loaded directly to the computer's hard drive and reviewed in flight. The ability to review photos within seconds after collection greatly improved our efficiency, as we could quickly tell if a photo pass was successful and repeat the pass if necessary. The rapid feedback provided by digital photography also eliminated concerns about exposure and focus that are common to film photography.

Survey aircraft

We used an Aero Commander 690B turbine engine aircraft owned and operated by Commander Northwest of Wenatchee, Washington to conduct our surveys (Figure 2). The aircraft was equipped with bubble windows which provided excellent lateral and downward visibility for walrus observations.

Figure 2. Aero Commander 690B turbine engine aircraft.

Flight crew

Field work was carried out by a four-person flight crew (Figure 3). The location of crew members and the configuration of the remote sensing systems in the aircraft are presented in Figure 4.

Figure 3. Survey flight crew. Pictured left to right are: William Baker (scanner operator), Douglas Burn (walrus observer and flight coordinator), Marc Webber (walrus observer and camera operator), and Ralph Aiken (pilot).

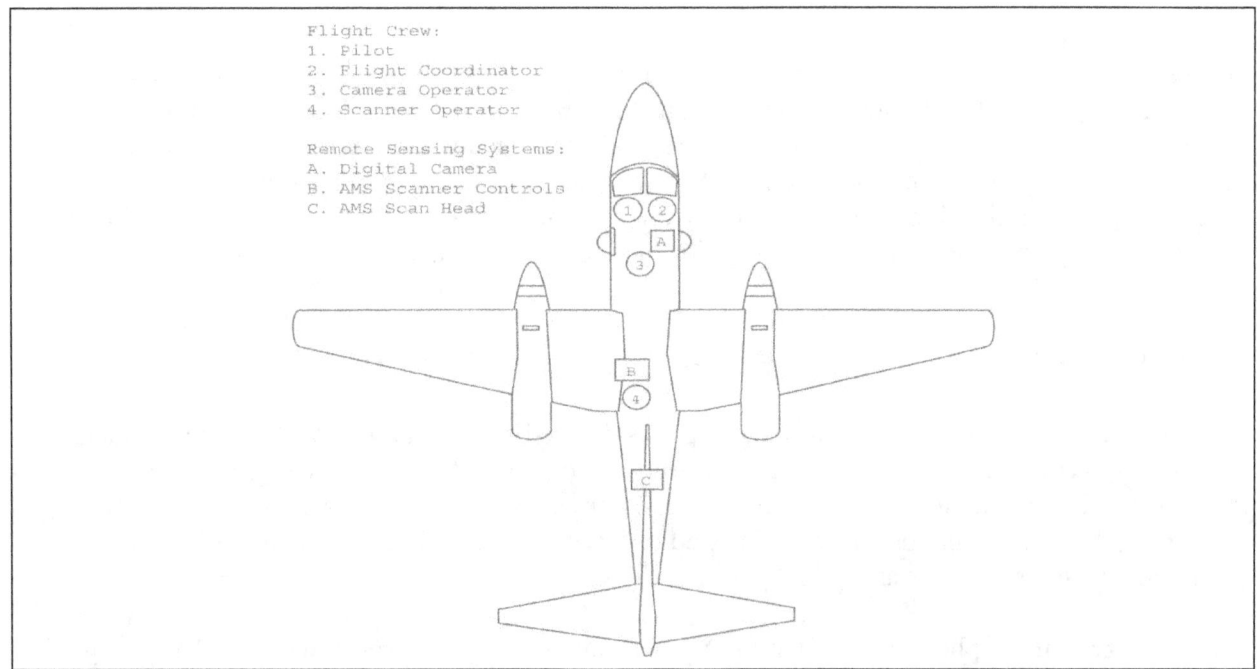

Figure 4. Diagram of survey aircraft indicating the location of flight crew and the configuration of the remote sensing systems.

Flight operations

Block selection for a given day was driven by local weather conditions. Cloud cover and cloud ceiling were instrumental in selecting which survey blocks to be flown. Once a block was identified, randomly selected transects (Figure 1) were entered into the aircraft's GPS for the day's mission.

Survey transects were flown at 3,200 m above ground level (AGL- all altitudes are reported as AGL), with an effective swath width of 6 km and a ground sampling resolution of 4 m (Burn *et al*. 2006). Turns and transits between transects were made as efficiently as possible to maximize the amount of survey effort. For each transect, the scanner operator recorded the transect number, start and finish times, ground speed, altitude, aircraft heading and the temperature of the scanner's two black bodies. To minimize the risk of data loss, each transect was stored and processed as a separate file, and the system and storage media were checked at the start of each new file.

After completing the survey transects, we descended to 762 m to collect digital aerial photographs from a subset of the "hotspots" identified with the thermal scanner. Photographs were taken using a 180 mm camera lens which produced an effective ground resolution of 3.4 cm^2 pixels. This resolution was sufficient to resolve and count individual walruses within a group (Burn *et al*. 2006), and was achieved from an altitude at which disturbance to resting animals was minimized. A Garmin GPS 3 was linked to the camera through a dedicated port, and aircraft position and exposure time were annotated to the metadata of each photograph. At the end of each flight day, we archived the digital photographs on compact disc media and an external hard drive.

In some cases digital photographs of walrus groups and corresponding thermal imagery were collected opportunistically during transit flights to or from the survey blocks. As walrus groups were sighted and photographed in the same general areas on consecutive days, it is possible that some of these sightings were duplicative. We considered these photographs appropriate for examining the relationship between walrus group size and thermal signature, but did not include any data in our analysis of abundance that was not collected on a survey transect.

Analytical methods

For the purpose of this study, a walrus group was defined as an aggregation of walruses on an ice floe lying in contact with or near to each other. We considered any walrus aggregations (including single animals) within 20 m of each other as a single group. Walruses in the water, including those that were partially submerged or resting head-up in a breathing hole in the ice, were not considered in our analysis.

We analyzed digital photographs of walrus groups and the AMS imagery with ERDAS Imagine (Leica Geosystems, Atlanta, Georgia) software. To count the number of walruses in a group, we created annotation layers and manually marked each walrus with a brightly colored symbol. Each walrus group was enumerated three times on different dates (without referring back to previous counts) using a different colored symbol each time. Finally, all three count layers were displayed simultaneously to compare the individual counts and arrive at a final, rectified count for each group.

We imported the AMS imagery directly from 8 mm tape into Imagine software using the Daedelus import module which corrects for distortion in the final image. To determine the threshold temperature value between walrus and the background environment we examined a frequency histogram of temperature values in the entire image. Within each image, the first histogram bin containing zero pixels was chosen as the temperature threshold value (Figure 5). The temperature histogram of an image typically contains one or more modal peaks which correspond to the predominant features in the image, such as thick, snow-covered ice, and thin, bare ice.

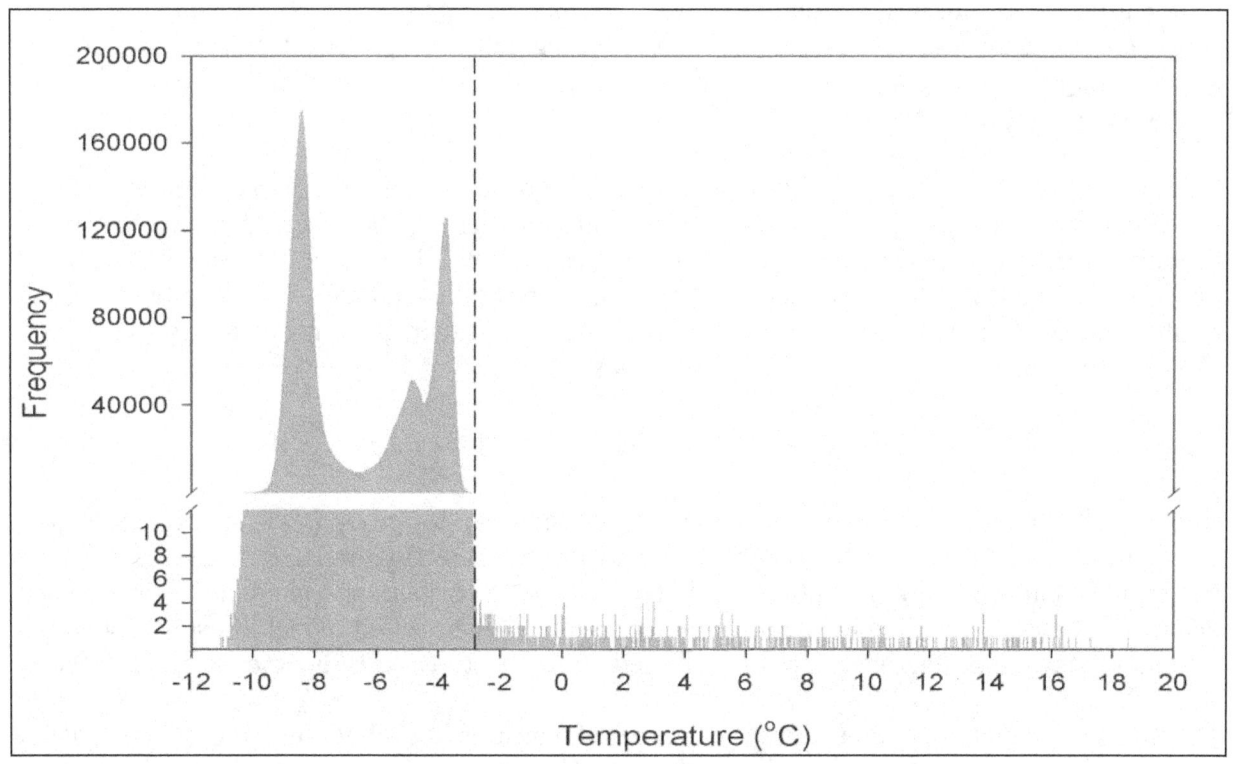

Figure 5. Example of frequency histogram of AMS thermal imagery showing temperature threshold between the background environment and walruses that occurs at -2.81°C. Pixels to the right of the threshold value have some portion of their area covered by walruses. The major peaks of the histogram correspond to environmental features such as thick, snow-covered ice, and bare ice of varying thickness.

Pixels with temperatures warmer than the threshold value were classified as having some portion of their area covered by walruses. After determining the threshold temperature for each image, we calculated an index of the total amount of heat produced by each walrus group as:

$$h_i = a \sum (t_{ij} - T_i),$$

where h_i was the index for group i, a was the pixel area (m^2), t_{ij} was the temperature for pixel j of group i, T_i was the threshold temperature for group i, and the summation was over all pixels with temperature values above the threshold (i.e., pixels with $t_{ij} > T_i$).

We estimated the scanner's detection limit based on photographic counts for the smallest thermally detected walrus groups, and the largest groups that were not thermally detected. There were 6 groups, ranging in size from 1 to 4 walruses that were photographed but were not detectable in the thermal imagery. The smallest photographed groups that were detected in thermal imagery contained 4 walruses (2 groups). We therefore assumed that groups with less than 4 walruses were not detectable.

Data from all of the photographed groups were used to develop a regression model relating group size to the thermal index. Preliminary examination of the data indicated that variances of the photographic counts were proportional to the mean counts. Therefore, we used a generalized linear model (McCullagh and Nelder 1989) with an identity link and a Poisson distribution to estimate the relation between numbers of individuals and the thermal index values for the photographed groups. The form of this model was:

$$E(y_i) = \alpha + \beta h_i, \quad Var(y_i) = \varphi(\alpha + \beta h_i),$$

where y_i is the number of walruses and h_i is the thermal index for group i, α is the minimum size group that can be detected by the scanner (i.e., the scanner detection limit), β is the regression coefficient estimated with maximum likelihood, and φ is the dispersion parameter estimated as Pearson's chi square divided by the degrees of freedom. We assessed model fit using deviance residuals (McCullagh and Nelder 1989) and used a Wald test to assess the regression parameter.

This model was then used to estimate the number of walruses in each thermally detected group on a surveyed transect that was not photographed. The total number of hauled-out walruses on a surveyed transect was estimated by summing the counts of individuals in all the photographed groups and the estimated counts in all the detected groups that were not photographed on that transect. For transect t in block b:

$$\hat{N}_{tb} = \sum_{g=1}^{c_{tb}} y_{gtb} + \sum_{g=c_{tb}+1}^{G_{tb}} (\alpha + \hat{\beta} h_{gtb}),$$

where y_{gtb} is the number of walruses in group g on transect t of block b, photographed groups are indexed $1, \ldots, c_{tb}$, and groups that were not photographed are indexed $c_{tb}+1, \ldots, G_{tb}$. If there were no photographed groups on a transect, then $c_{tb} = 0$.

The total population size was estimated as a sum of separate ratio estimators (Cochran 1977) of the totals for each survey block:

$$\hat{N} = \sum_{b=1}^{B} \left(\hat{R}_b \sum_{t=1}^{T_b} A_{tb} \right) = \sum_{b=1}^{B} \hat{N}_b ,$$

where:

$$\hat{R}_b = \frac{\sum_{t=1}^{t_b} \hat{N}_{tb}}{\sum_{t=1}^{t_b} A_{tb}} ,$$

A_{tb} is the area of transect t in block b, T_b is the number of transects in block b, t_b is the number of surveyed transects in block b, and B is the number of survey blocks.

We estimated variance of the population estimate with a bootstrap (Efron 1982) procedure based on the general approach of Booth *et al.* (1994) for finite populations. The procedure involved generating of series of simulated populations, estimating statistics of interest by resampling from each simulated population, and then averaging these statistics over the simulated populations.

We generated simulated populations of transects (with associated walrus observations) for each block by first replicating the complete set of surveyed transects in the block as many times as possible without exceeding the total number of potential transects in the block. We then added a random sample without replacement from the surveyed transects to complete the population of potential transects. Bootstrap survey samples were obtained by drawing random samples without replacement from the simulated populations to give the same number of transects as in the original survey.

For each bootstrap survey sample, we also obtained a bootstrap sample of photographic counts for fitting the regression model. A bootstrap sample of photographed groups included all of the photographed groups in the bootstrap sample of surveyed transects if the number of those groups was ≤ the number on surveyed transects in the original sample. Otherwise, we sampled without replacement from the photographed groups in the bootstrap sample of transects to obtain the same number as in the original survey. We then completed the bootstrap sample of photographed groups by sampling with replacement from the entire original sample of groups photographed off survey transects to obtain the same total sample size (i.e., number of groups photographed on transects + number of groups photographed off transects) as in the original survey. This resampling strategy was designed to approximate the survey protocol which supplemented the essentially random distribution of group sizes photographed on survey transects with additional off-transect photographs emphasizing larger groups, thereby obtaining a more even distribution of group sizes for the calibration regression.

Estimation for each bootstrap sample followed the same procedure as for the original sample. We obtained 100 bootstrap samples and associated estimates of population size for each simulated population and then calculated the standard error and 2.5 and 97.5 percentiles of those estimates. We repeated this process for 500 simulated populations and took the average of the standard errors and 2.5 and 97.5 percentiles as our estimates of standard errors and 95% confidence limits for the estimates from the original survey.

Results

During the two-week field period we were able collect data on six consecutive days (April 5-10) and were able to survey six of seven survey blocks. Block 5 (Figure 1) was missed due to a technical problem encountered with the scanner system on April 11. After April 11, weather conditions deteriorated, and we were unable to fly again during the remainder of our deployment. We sampled a total area of 28,875 km^2 with the AMS system at a spatial resolution of 4 m, and encountered many walrus groups scattered throughout the survey area (Figure 1).

Survey effort is summarized in Table 1. Survey efficiency, measured as the proportion of the survey block sampled with the AMS system, ranged from 21 to 38 percent. The number of square kilometers scanned per day ranged from 3,622 to 6,051 with a mean of 4,813. Air speed, which ranged from 333 to 444 km/hr, was not limited by scanner operations but was affected by wind speed and direction.

During the 2003 survey effort, threshold temperatures ranged from -2.98 to -4.32 °C. In general, the threshold temperatures were lower when ambient temperatures were lower. We photographed a total of 46 walrus groups during the survey period and were able to match 25 of these to corresponding hotspots in the thermal imagery. Walrus group sizes and their corresponding thermal values are presented in Table 2. Thermal values for all walrus hotspots recorded during the survey are presented in Appendix 2. There was a strong linear relationship (X_1^2 =90.02, $P <$ 0.01) between the numbers of walruses in a group and the index of total walrus heat (Figure 6), with a slope parameter estimate of $\beta = 0.67$ (standard error = 0.0070). Plots of deviance residuals did not show any lack of fit to the linear model or the Poisson variance function.

Abundance estimates for survey blocks are presented in Table 3. The total number of walruses in the 6 surveyed blocks was estimated at 4,785 animals with a standard error of 1,186 (C.V. = 0.25) and a 95 % confidence interval of 2,499–7,111.

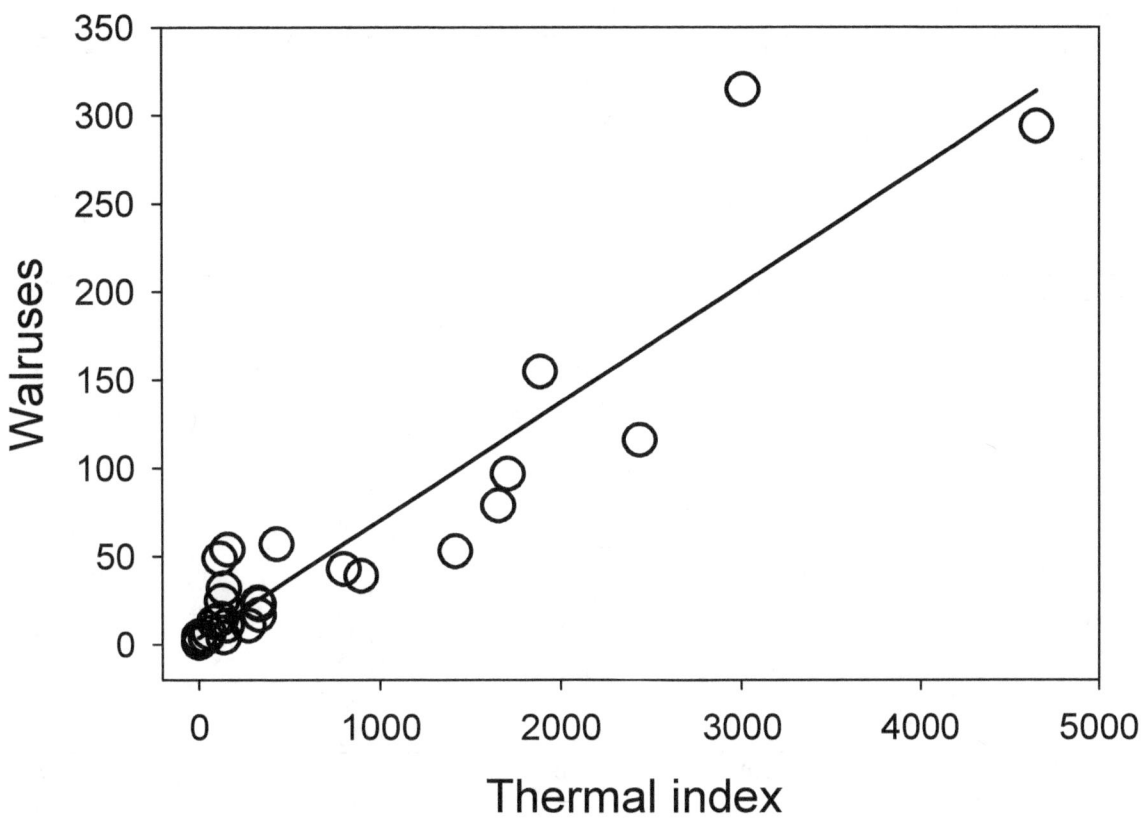

Figure 6. Poisson regression of walrus counts as a function of total heat index for AMS thermal imagery at 4 m spatial resolution. See text for model details.

During flight operations we observed, but were unable to photograph, several small flocks of birds. We also observed and photographed several seals (*Phoca spp.* or bearded seal *Erignathus barbatus*). No bird aggregations or seals could be confirmed in the scanner data, probably because they presented too small of a thermal target at the four meter resolution obtained at 3,200 m.

Table 1. Survey blocks and transects flown.

Date	Block	Block Area (km²)	Transect	Transect Length (km)	Sampled Area [a] (km²)
4/05/2003	3	18,455	452	105.9	635.7
			455	113.2	679.1
			456	112.9	677.5
			458	112.1	672.8
			459	189.8	1,138.7
			466	142.5	854.8
			Subtotal	**776.4**	**4,658.4**
4/06/2003	7	15,900	356	144.1	864.9
			358	142.8	857.0
			360	145.2	871.4
			363	143.4	860.6
			364	144.1	864.9
			366	144.7	868.2
			368	144.2	865.4
			Subtotal	**1,008.5**	**6,051.0**
4/07/2003	2	15,903	437	176.8	1,060.9
			438	180.7	1,083.9
			446	191.7	1,150.5
			447	190.9	1,145.1
			449	190.3	1,141.8
			Subtotal	**930.4**	**5,582.4**
4/08/2003	1	13,808	416	65.3	391.8
			419	52.9	317.6
			420	64.1	384.6
			422	86.4	518.5
			424	100.8	605.0
			425	109.0	653.9
			426	115.4	692.3
			430	123.3	739.9
			Subtotal	**717.2**	**4,303.2**
4/09/2003	6	15,310	336	107.6	645.5
			337	107.9	647.5
			339	127.0	762.3
			345	144.5	866.7
			347	144.4	866.4
			350	144.9	869.2
			Subtotal	**776.3**	**4,657.8**
4/10/2003	4	17,525	314	213.6	1,281.7
			315	224.7	1,348.0
			312	165.4	992.4
			Subtotal	**603.7**	**3,622.2**
Total				**4,812.5**	**28,875.0**

[a] Sampled Area (km²) is equal to transect length (km) multiplied by the scanner swath width (6 km).

Table 2. Total walrus heat measured for each walrus hotspot recorded with corresponding walrus counts from digital aerial photography.

Date	Total Walrus Heat	Walrus Count
4/07/2003	797.62	43
	329.47	17
	427.78	57
	329.47	23
	1,887.07	155
4/08/2003	39.70	4
	135.30	4
	4,652.21	294
	127.40	25
	3,006.84	315
4/09/2003	157.64	54
	113.52	49
	137.75	32
4/10/2003	84.08	13
	1.07	5
	271.71	11
	54.74	7
	120.93	15
	1,704.84	97
	322.61	24
	893.64	39
	2,436.68	116
	152.24	11
	1,413.85	53
	1,651.65	79

Table 3. Abundance estimates for survey blocks.

Block	Total Walruses	Standard Error	95% Conf. Interval
1	424	166	131–761
2	2,057	846	395–3693
3	509	349	40–1252
4	1,278	509	555–2259
6	505	317	3–1050
7	12	9	0–29

Discussion

Objective 1. Conduct a full operational test of the AMS system to evaluate the potential of this
        system as a survey tool for Pacific walruses distributed over a wide geographic area

The development of an aerial survey method using thermal imaging technology would address
many of the shortcomings of visual aerial surveys described by Gilbert (1999). Visual surveys
have historically been flown at relatively low altitudes (150-300 m) and airspeeds (250 km/hr)
that allowed for both detection and counting of walrus groups in a relatively narrow swath,
usually 1.86 km or less. The proportion of the study area that could be searched by visual
methods was typically low, resulting in population estimates of low precision (Estes and Gilbert
1978, Gilbert 1999). By flying at a higher altitude (3,200 m) and at faster airspeeds (370 km/hr),
and using a thermal scanner with an effective swath width of 6 km to detect walrus groups, it is
theoretically possible to sample up to 400% more area per hour of flight time than with
traditional visually based survey methods (Burn *et al.* 2006).

Our operational test of the AMS system indicated that walrus groups > 4 animals were readily
detected at a spatial resolution of 4 m. Walrus range in size from 1-3 m, and we suspect that
individual animals and small groups may have been missed at this spatial resolution. Walruses
are extremely gregarious animals and normally haul out on ice floes in large groups (Fay 1982).
We found that most (94.6%) of the walruses photographed during the survey occurred in groups
> 6 animals. Results of previous visual aerial surveys also indicate that walruses typically occur
in group sizes that would be detectable at this spatial resolution (Estes and Gilbert 1978, Garlich-
Miller and Jay 2000; Burn *et al.* 2006), therefore we consider the magnitude of any bias due to
undetected groups to be relatively small.

The 95% confidence interval for the number of walruses hauled out in the 6 surveyed blocks of
our study area was 2,499 -7,111 animals. It is important to point out that this abundance estimate
does not account for animals in the water during the survey. Developing a correction factor for
walruses in the water during our aerial survey was beyond the scope of this project. Recently,
Jay *et al. (*2006) have developed satellite radio transmitter tags for walruses that record wet and
dry intervals from which correction factors for aerial surveys can be developed. These tags can
be deployed with crossbows, and are attached to animals via a harpoon head lodged underneath
the skin. USGS is currently modeling telemetry data collected in 2004 and 2005 to estimate the
number of tags necessary to deploy in support of a range wide population survey (Udevitz *et al.*
2004). Data collected during this pilot survey is being used along with the telemetry data to
estimate the amount of survey effort necessary to obtain an abundance estimate for the Pacific
walrus population with an acceptable level of precision (Udevitz *et al.* 2004, USFWS and USGS
In prep).

We believe that the AMS system as configured for this study would be a highly effective tool for
surveying large areas of sea ice habitat for walrus groups. With a 6 km swath width, it should be
possible to sample more than 10,000 km^2 in an 8-hr flight. The system could theoretically be
flown at higher altitudes with larger spatial resolutions, covering an even larger area; however,
the proportion of the walrus population that would be missed would also increase. Alternatively,

as systems with smaller IFOVs and larger pixel arrays become available, it may be possible to survey larger areas with the same 4 m resolution. Based on the results and experience gained during this pilot survey, the USFWS contracted with ArgonST to build a detector with a 0.625 milliradian IFOV and 3,000 pixel array. This system, tested in the spring of 2005, generated 4 m spatial resolution data with a swath width of approximately 12 km from edge to edge when flown at 6,400 m. Additionally, at this altitude, the 690B Turbine Commander was considerably more fuel efficient and could cruise at speeds up to 463 km/hr. These factors combined to increase survey efficiency by roughly 250% over the results obtained in this study (USFWS, unpublished data).

In addition to thermal imagery, high-resolution digital photographs, suitable for counting individual walruses, need to be obtained from a representative sample of walrus groups to allow estimation of group sizes from the thermal data. Given the relative importance of large walrus groups to the overall number of walruses observed, it is important to photograph the full range of walrus group sizes. We recommend a double-sampling design (Thompson 2002) in which a random sample of survey transects are scanned using the AMS system and a random sample of the thermally detected walrus groups photographed. Based upon the experience gained in this study, and in consideration of the cost in fuel and flight time associated with repeatedly changing altitudes between scanner operation (3,200 m) and photography (762 m), we recommend that a separate (second) aircraft be deployed to collect photographs. The scanner and photography airplanes could work together at different altitudes and relay information back and forth by radio or satellite phone on the position and size of groups to enhance the effectiveness of data collection.

Although we believe this test survey demonstrates the utility of airborne thermal imagery in surveys of Pacific walrus, additional field work conducted under extremely cold conditions in April 2005 indicated that the ability to detect walrus groups in thermal imagery is in part a function of ambient temperatures. Based on these results, we are exploring alternative analytical procedures for identifying walrus groups in thermal imagery, as well as alternative calculations of thermal index values that accounts for variations in ambient temperature. In addition to the apparent influence of ambient temperature on detection of walrus groups, the requirement of cloud-free conditions may also be a limiting factor for survey operations. An analysis of historical weather information should be incorporated into any study plan for surveying the Pacific walrus population.

Based on the success of this pilot survey and recent innovations in satellite telemetry packages capable of tracking walrus movements and haulout patterns (Jay et al. 2006) the USFWS and USGS, in cooperation with Russian scientists, have begun to develop a study plan for a range-wide survey of the Pacific walrus population (USFWS and USGS 2006). The study plan outlines an operational strategy to estimate the size of the Pacific walrus population using an AMS system and digital photography. The proposed survey would occur in spring, when the Pacific walrus population is distributed near the southern edge of the Bering Sea ice pack. Prior to the aerial survey, satellite transmitters would be deployed on a representative sample of walruses distributed across Bering Sea pack ice. The transmitters would record the proportion of time each tagged walrus is hauled out on the ice or in the water and this information used to develop a correction factor for animals not detected during the aerial survey (Udevitz 2005).

Objective 2. Evaluate the effectiveness of the AMS system as a survey tool for other marine
   mammal and bird species

We had limited success evaluating the AMS system as a survey tool for other marine mammal or
bird species in the study area. We had intended to systematically search the area for other
pinniped and bird species and collect thermal imagery from a variety of spatial resolutions in
order to evaluate the capability of the AMS system in detecting and enumerating these species.
Unfortunately, weather conditions deteriorated towards the end of our study period and we were
unable to complete this aspect of the mission.

Our survey effort for walrus groups was conducted from 3,200 m with a ground sample
resolution of 4 m. The tendency for walruses to aggregate into large groups permits sampling at
this relatively course resolution with its correspondingly broad swath width (Burn *et al.* 2006).
While the 4 m spatial resolution is sufficient for detecting and enumerating walrus groups, it
apparently is insufficient for detecting individual seals. During our walrus survey effort, we
sighted and were able to photograph several single seals *(Phoca spp.* and *Erignathus barbatus)*
from an altitude of 762 m. None of these seals were detected in the corresponding 4 m thermal
data. Large flocks of spectacled eiders are known to occur in the study area (Petersen *et al.*
1999); however we did not encounter any aggregations during our surveys.

Theoretically, the AMS system should be capable of detecting any endothermic species in an ice
environment providing that there is sufficient resolution to detect the thermal contrast between
the target and its back ground. Unfortunately, flying at lower altitudes to obtain a greater
resolution will also reduce the area covered by the scanner, and affect the utility of the scanner as
a survey tool. We also anticipate challenges in distinguishing between species that are similar in
size unless the target species selects unique habitat features or has striking and consistent
behavioral attributes such as group size or configuration.

Acknowledgments

We thank the other members of our survey team, Ralph Aiken and William Baker, for their skill
and expertise during the field portion of this study. David Weintraub (Commander Northwest)
was instrumental in ensuring the survey aircraft would meet the necessary specifications. Fred
Osterwisch, Tom Ory, and Jason Jester (ArgonST) provided valuable technical support for the
AMS system. Jan Bennett, Lark Wuerth, and Bud Walters (U.S. Department of Interior Office
of Aircraft Services) insured that the study was conducted in accordance with safety guidelines.
We also thank staff from the National Weather Service in Nome, Alaska for their assistance with
weather forecasts and mission planning. This study was conducted under U.S. Department of
Interior Letter of Confirmation MA-039582.

Study Products

Reports and publications

Burn, D., M. Webber and M. Udevitz. (2006). Application of airborne thermal imagery to surveys of Pacific walrus *Odobenus rosmarus divergens*). Wildlife Society Bulletin 34:51–58.

Udevitz, M.S. 2005. Statistical procedures for estimating Pacific walrus population size. Technical report, Alaska Science Center, U.S. Geological Survey, Anchorage, Alaska. 9 pp.

USFWS and USGS. (2006.) Study Plan for estimating the size of the Pacific walrus population.

Udevitz, M.S., D.M. Burn and M.A. Webber. (*In prep*) Estimation of walrus populations on sea ice with infrared imagery and aerial photography.

Presentations

Burn, D., M. Webber and M. Udevitz. 2003. Application of Airborne Thermal Remote Sensing to Surveys of Pacific walrus (*Odobenus rosmarus divergens*). *Presented at:* 15th Biennial Conference on the Biology of Marine Mammals, 14-19 December, Greensboro NC.

Burn, D., M. Webber and M. Udevitz. 2004.. Using Airborne Thermal Remote Sensing to Survey Pacific walrus (*Odobenus rosmarus divergens*) *Presented at:* Marine Mammals of the Holarctic III, 11-17 October, Koktebel, Ukraine.

Udevitz, M. S., D. B. Burn, A. S. Fischbach, C. V. Jay, and M. A. Webber. 2004. Survey design for estimating Pacific walrus population size. *Presented at:* Marine Mammals of the Holarctic III, 11-17 October, Koktebel, Ukraine.

Literature Cited

Barber, D.G., P.R. Richard, R. P. Hochheim, and J. Orr. 1991. Calibration of aerial thermal infrared imagery for walrus population assessment. Arctic. 44(supp. 1):58-65.

Booth, J.G., Butler, R.W., and Hall, P. 1994. Bootstrap methods for finite populations. Journal of the American Statistical Association 89(428):1282-1289.

Burn, D., M. Webber and M. Udevitz. (2006). Application of airborne thermal imagery to surveys of Pacific walrus *Odobenus rosmarus divergens*). Wildlife Society Bulletin 34:51–58. .

Cochran, W.G. 1977. Sampling techniques, third edition. John Wiley & Sons, New York.

Cressie, N. 1991. Statistics for spatial data. John Wiley & Sons, New York.

Efron, B. 1982. The jackknife, the bootstrap and other resampling plans. Society for Industrial and Applied Mathematics, Philadelphia, Pennsylvania.

Estes, J.A. and J.R. Gilbert. 1978. Evaluation of an aerial survey of Pacific walruses (*Odobenus rosmarus divergens*). Journal of the Fisheries Research Board of Canada 35:1130-1140.

Fay, F.H. 1982. Ecology and biology of the Pacific walrus, *Odobenus rosmarus divergens Illiger*. North American Fauna. No. 74.

Fay, F.H., and G.C. Ray. 1968. Influence of climate on the distribution of walruses, *Odobenus rosmarus Linnaeus*. I. Evidence from thermoregulatory behavior. Zoologica, 53:1-14.

Garlich-Miller, J. and C.V Jay. 2000. Proceedings of a workshop concerning walrus survey methods. USFWS R7/MMM Technical Report 00-2, 92 pp.

Gilbert, J.R. 1999. Review of previous Pacific walrus surveys to develop improved survey designs. *In*: Garner, G.W., S.C. Amstrup, J.L. Laake, B.F.J. Manly, L.L. McDonald, and D.G. Robertson *(EDS.)*, Marine Mammal Survey and Assessment Methods. A. A. Balkema, Rotterdam, 287 pp.

Gilbert, J.R., G.A. Fedoseev, D. J. Seagars, E. Razlivalov, and A. LaChugin. 1992. Aerial census of Pacific walrus, 1990. USFWS R7/MMM Technical Report 92-1, 33 pp.

Hills, S. and J.R. Gilbert. 1994. Detecting Pacific walrus population trends with aerial survey - a review. Transactions North American Wildlife and Natural Resource Conference.

Jay, C.V., M.P. Heide-Jørgensen, A.S. Fischbach, M.V. Jensen, D.F. Tessler, and A.V. Jensen. (2006). Comparison of remotely deployed satellite radio transmitters on walruses. Marine Mammal Science. 22:226–236.

McCullagh, P. and Nelder, J.A. 1989. Generalized linear models, second edition. Chapman and Hall, Boca Raton, Florida.

Petersen, M.R., Larned, W. W., and Douglas, D. C. 1999. At-sea distribution of spectacled eiders: A 120-year-old mystery resolved. Auk 116:1009-1020.

Ray, G.C. and F.H. Fay. 1968. Influence of climate on the distribution of walruses, *Odobenus rosmarus Linnaeus*. II. Evidence from physiological characteristics. Zoologia, 53:19-32.

Thompson, S. K. 2002. Sampling. John Wiley & Sons, New York, New York.

Udevitz, M.S. 2005. Statistical procedures for estimating Pacific walrus population size. Technical report, Alaska Science Center, U.S. Geological Survey, Anchorage, Alaska. 9 pp.

Udevitz, M. S., D. B. Burn, A. S. Fischbach, C. V. Jay, and M. A. Webber. 2004. Survey design for estimating Pacific walrus population size. Abstract of paper presented at Marine Mammals of the Holarctic III, 11-17 October, Koktebel, Ukraine.

Udevitz, M.S., J.R. Gilbert, and G.A. Fedoseev. 2001. Comparison of the methods used to estimate numbers of walruses on sea ice. Marine Mammal Science 17(3):601-616.

Wartzok, D., and G.C. Ray. 1980. The hauling-out behavior of the Pacific walrus. U.S. Marine Mammal Commission Report MMC-75/15. 46pp.

Wolter, K.M. 1984. An investigation of some estimators of variance for systematic sampling. Journal of the American Statistical Association 79(388):781-790.

Appendix 1. Scanner specifications

AMS *Airborne Multispectral Scanner*

The AMS system is a dual optical port multispectral scanner which records up to six spectral channels simultaneously directly onto an 8 mm digital tape. The AMS provides calibrated thermal information for the determination of radiometric temperature relationships for various remote sensing applications. The compact scan head and electronics can be installed in a wide range of aircraft using standard 16" aerial camera ports and seat assemblies.

The standard sensor configuration offers a dual element thermal infrared detector and an 8-channel, visible/near infrared spectrometer so that a total of 10 spectral bands are available. Up to six of these bands may be selected for recording by the operator. An ultraviolet detector/dichroic assembly may be substituted for the spectrometer to expand system capabilities.

The system's Built-In Test (BIT) capabilities deliver a high level of confidence in mission success. An on-board image display provides a real-time check of flight line coverage and data quality. A built-in differential ready GPS receiver automatically inserts navigation data into the housekeeping message in the header of each scan line.

The AMS provides operator control via a menu-driven touch screen. An optional printer can provide continuous real-time hard copy images plus a VHS video recording can be made from the monitor output.

AMS data tapes may be read and processed by ERDAS Imagine® image processing software, using the "Daedalus" importer.

The AMS collects data for applications as diverse as:

- Geologic mapping
- Forest inventory
- Fire mapping
- Oil spill detection/mapping
- Water chlorophyll studies
- And many more.

System photo depicts one variation of system.

■ Digital performance – 8-bit and 12-bit resolution
■ Ten spectral channels

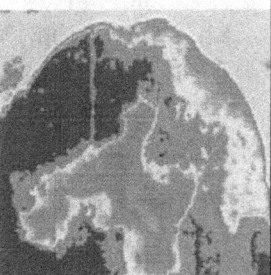

Bay Environment Study shows sea water pollution, suspended solids and chlorophyll conditions. *(Courtesy Asia Air Survey Company, Ltd., Japan)*

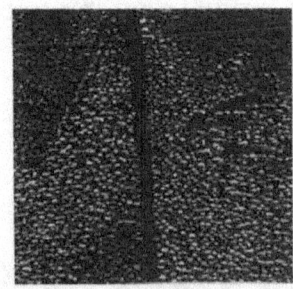

Acid Rain Study of a forest area shows degradation of healthy trees over a one year period. Red dots are dead trees. *(Courtesy Eurosense, Belgium)*

Imagery of waste settling ponds in the San Francisco Bay area shows dramatic differences in spectral signatures. Diked ponds, some of which are used for industrial processing wastes, require airborne monitoring to detect leakage. *(Courtesy of NASA/Ames Research Center) NASA does not endorse any commercial product.*

Imaging Group

Environmental Remote Sensing Technology

AMS *Airborne Multispectral Scanner*

PARTIAL LISTING OF APPLICATIONS:

PARTIAL LISTING OF APPLICATIONS:	UV	1	2	3	4	5	6	7	8	3-5 μm SWIR	8.5-12.5 μm LWIR
Geologic Mapping			X	X		X		X		X	X
Water Chlorophyll		X		X					X		X
Water Suspended Sediment				X				X			X
Water Temperature								X			X
Forest Inventory		X	X	X	X		X	X			
Crop Vigor Studies		X	X		X		X				X
Fire Detection/Mapping										X	X
Oil Spill Detection/Mapping	X									X	X

(Header spanning: SPECTRAL BANDS; VIS/NIR Spectrometer Channels covers columns 1–8)

Examples of typical applications and their recommended spectral combinations are depicted in the chart above.

OPTIONS

DETECTORS
Ultraviolet Detector (UV), 320 - 380 nm (5.0 mrad only)
8 Band CZCS Array Assembly

(**Note:** Detectors can be purchased later as needs develop.)

HARDCOPY PRINTER
Continuous hardcopy image of raw video data (corrected for s-bend and V/H geometric distortions)

DETECTOR CRYO-COOLING

INSTALLATION ASSISTANCE

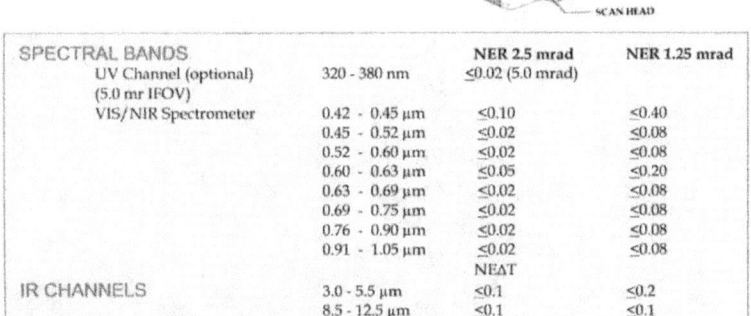

DATA RECORDER MONITOR
DIGITIZER
POWER DISTRIBUTOR
SCAN HEAD

SPECTRAL BANDS		NER 2.5 mrad	NER 1.25 mrad
UV Channel (optional) (5.0 mr IFOV)	320 - 380 nm	≤0.02 (5.0 mrad)	
VIS/NIR Spectrometer	0.42 - 0.45 μm	≤0.10	≤0.40
	0.45 - 0.52 μm	≤0.02	≤0.08
	0.52 - 0.60 μm	≤0.02	≤0.08
	0.60 - 0.63 μm	≤0.05	≤0.20
	0.63 - 0.69 μm	≤0.02	≤0.08
	0.69 - 0.75 μm	≤0.02	≤0.08
	0.76 - 0.90 μm	≤0.02	≤0.08
	0.91 - 1.05 μm	≤0.02	≤0.08
		NEΔT	
IR CHANNELS	3.0 - 5.5 μm	≤0.1	≤0.2
	8.5 - 12.5 μm	≤0.1	≤0.1

NER is μW/cm²nmsr and NEΔT in °C (6.25 scans/sec)

PHYSICAL SPECIFICATIONS

	Height in	cm	Width in	cm	Depth* in	cm
Scan Head	15.0	38.0	15.0	38.0	15.0	38.0
Electronics	28.0	71.2	20.0	50.8	20.0	50.8

	lbs	kg
Total System Weight (approx.)	185	84

* Depth not including connectors and cables

ENVIRONMENTAL SPECIFICATIONS

	Temperature	Rel. Humidity (non-condensing)	Altitude
Scan Head	-55° to +70°C	0 - 95%	50,000 ft (15,200 m)
Electronics (operating)	+5° to +40°C	20 - 80%	25,000 ft* (7,600 m)
Electronics (non-operating)	-40° to +60°C	0 - 95%	50,000 ft (15,200 m)

* Video monitor will automatically switch off above 14,500 ft (4,400 m)

TECHNICAL SPECIFICATIONS

INSTANTANEOUS FIELD OF VIEW
2.5 milliradians (1.25 mrad optional)

DIGITIZED FIELD OF VIEW – 86°
720 pixels @ 2.5 mrad
1440 pixels @ 1.25 mrad

SCAN RATES
100, 50, 25, 12.5, 6.25 scans/sec
(operator selectable)

VELOCITY/HEIGHT RATIO (V/H)
0.25 radians/sec @ 100 scans/sec @ 2.5 mrad IFOV; 0.125 radians/sec @ 1.25 mrad IFOV

ROLL CORRECTION
±15° of roll correction (automatic)

POWER REQUIREMENTS
28 ±3 VDC, 30 amps continuous (not including optional hardcopy printer)

IMAGE DISPLAY
9" CRT (640 pixels wide in continuous moving window, RS-170/CCIR output)

DIGITIZATION PRECISION
8-bit or 12-bit (operator selectable)

DATA RECORDING LIMITS
(12-bit words)
4 channels @ 1.25 mrad 100 scans/sec
6 channels @ all other resolutions and scan speeds
(8-bit words, 1.25 or 2.5 mrad)
6 channels maximum @ all scan speeds

RECORD TIME AT 100 SCANS/SEC
(2 channel operation)

2.5 mrad	1.25 mrad
12-bit - 6.2 hrs min	12-bit - 3.2 hrs min
8-bit - 9.2 hrs min	8-bit - 4.7 hrs min

THERMAL REFERENCE SOURCES
Two controllable field-filling blackbody reference sources. Range of -15° to +25°C with respect to scan head heat sink temperature.

GPS RECEIVER
A GPS receiver is integral to the system. Date, time, ground speed, latitude, longitude and track angle are recorded on the system data tape.

Rev. 3 - Nov. 2004

Imaging Group
P.O. Box 1869
Ann Arbor, MI 48106-1869 USA
(734) 769-5649 FAX (734) 769-0429

www.argonst.com
Corporate Headquarters
12701 Fair Lakes Circle, Suite 800, Fairfax, VA 22033
Phone (703) 322-0881 FAX (703) 322-0885

Appendix 2. Total walrus heat measured for each walrus hotspot recorded

Date	Transect Number [a]	Total Walrus Heat	Walrus Count
4/05/2003	452	68.79	
	452	45.98	
	452	572.82	
	452	391.05	
	452	209.76	
	452	8.48	
	459	84.61	
	466	55.03	
4/06/2003	366	5.46	
4/07/2003	437	20.66	
	438	19.96	
	446	10.90	
	446	23.67	
	446	6.89	
	446	52.80	
		71.69	
		8.84	
		797.62	43
		86.62	
		329.47	17
		9.03	
		97.47	
		58.70	
	447	51.69	
	447	578.04	
	447	45.04	
	447	340.23	
	447	3,818.46	
	449	760.65	
	449	59.89	
	449	78.28	
	449	52.97	
	449	427.78	57
	449	329.47	23
	449	304.78	
	449	10.91	
	449	1,887.07	155
4/08/2003	422	15.25	
	422	6.67	
	424	39.70	4
	424	363.66	
	424	78.53	
	424	135.30	4
	424	92.96	

Date	Transect Number [a]	Total Walrus Heat	Walrus Count
4/08/2003	424	79.85	
	424	10.74	
	425	161.64	
	425	105.81	
	426	13.82	
	426	105.94	
	426	9.06	
	426	26.88	
		208.00	
		4,652.21	294
		127.40	25
		3,006.84	315
4/09/2003	345	18.30	
	345	157.64	54
	345	3.31	
	345	113.52	49
	345	137.75	32
	347	6.46	
	347	1.54	
		26.00	
4/10/2003	312	7.99	
	312	18.91	
	312	84.08	13
	312	14.90	
	312	25.34	
	312	1.07	5
	314	28.46	
	314	6.99	
	314	5.04	
	314	3.26	
	314	11.56	
	314	26.71	
	314	8.55	
	314	107.66	
	314	43.76	
	314	29.80	
	314	1.10	
	314	62.92	
	314	11.22	
	314	79.81	
	314	28.78	
	314	5.59	
	314	53.41	
	314	1.11	
	314	22.50	

Date	Transect Number [a]	Total Walrus Heat	Walrus Count
4/10/2003	314	1.80	
	314	39.74	
	314	135.06	
	314	308.83	
	314	47.93	
	314	8.68	
	314	21.84	
	314	12.27	
	314	16.84	
	315	25.00	
	315	65.65	
	315	56.60	
	315	15.56	
	315	26.89	
	315	8.83	
	315	19.86	
		271.71	11
		695.27	
		11.93	
		156.71	
		557.54	
		198.29	
		25.59	
		54.74	7
		120.93	15
		1,704.84	97
		322.61	24
		893.64	39
		2,436.68	116
		152.24	11
		1.41	
		1,413.85	53
		4.57	
		72.89	
		0.80	
		1,651.65	79

[a] Hotspots with missing transect number were recorded supplemental to survey effort.

www.ingramcontent.com/pod-product-compliance
Lightning Source LLC
Chambersburg PA
CBHW080938290526
45795CB00007BA/2810